Prince Pantyhose

by Jean Ure
illustrated by Chris Mould

Contents

Chapter 1	3
Chapter 2	13
Chapter 3	22
Chapter 4	37
Chapter 5	54
Chapter 6	67

COTTESBROOKE JUNIOR SCHOOL
CEDARS AVENUE
BIRMINGHAM
B27 6JL

Text © Jean Ure 2003
Series editors: Martin Coles and Christine Hall

PEARSON EDUCATION LIMITED
Edinburgh Gate
Harlow
Essex CM20 2JE
England

www.longman.co.uk

The right of Jean Ure to be identified as the author of this work has been asserted by her in accordance with the Copyright, Designs and Patents Act, 1988.

All rights reserved. No part of this publication may be reproduced, stored in a retrieval system, or transmitted in any form or by any means, electronic, mechanical, photocopying, recording, or otherwise without either the prior written permission of the Publishers or a licence permitting restricted copying in the United Kingdom issued by the Copyright Licensing Agency Ltd, 90 Tottenham Court Road, London W1P 9HE.

First published 2003
ISBN 0582 79622 9

Illustrated by Chris Mould

Printed in Great Britain by Scotprint, Haddington

The publishers' policy is to use paper manufactured from sustainable forests.

Chapter 1

Once upon a time there was a king and a queen, and their son – who was, of course, a prince. They all lived in a castle, at the top of a hill, surrounded by members of the royal household. There were knights and barons, courtiers and clerics, ladies-in-waiting and gentlemen of the bedchamber – not to mention all the scullions and the minions, all the cooks and the grooms and the bottle-washers. The castle was a very busy place.

There was a mighty drawbridge which went up and down at least a dozen times a day, and a moat into which the cooks and the bottle-washers emptied their buckets, and the scullions and the minions tossed sticks and stones and bits of old food. The Master of the King's Household was forever telling them to stop doing it, but the Master of the King's Household was old and doddery, and the scullions and the minions took

CHAPTER ONE

no notice. The kitchen maids and serving wenches were rather better behaved, because the Chief Cook (who was very bad-tempered) threatened to smack their heads with a ladle if they dared do anything wrong. So mostly they didn't.

It was the Prince who did things wrong. He was even worse behaved than the lowest of the scullions and the minions; but being a prince, he could get away with it. No one told *him* not to throw stuff into the moat. No one threatened to smack *his* head with a ladle. The fact of the matter was that the Prince was a bit of a spoilt brat. It was true the Queen occasionally grew irritated and told the King to do something, but the King just said that boys would be boys, and princes would be princes, and that was all there was to it.

"He'll grow out of it, my dear."

"He'd better," snapped the Queen.

So far, the Prince showed no signs of doing so. Just the other week he had pelted the Abbot of Gobalot Abbey with bad eggs as the Abbot fatly progressed across the drawbridge. He had claimed it was an accident; but what was he doing with bad eggs in the first place?

"I could have used those in the pottage," grumbled the cook. "No one would ever have noticed."

She was right. Cook put all kinds of disgusting things in her pottage. Bad eggs, rotting vegetables, stinky old meat. Both the King and the Queen were a bit frightened of her, owing to her extreme bad temper, so they never said anything; just meekly picked at whatever she gave them.

"Waste of good bad eggs," grumbled Cook.

The eggs had scored a direct hit on top of the Abbot's head. He had smelled perfectly foul for days.

"Oh, Panty!" sighed the Queen. "What are we to do with you?"

Panty was her pet name for the Prince. His real name was Pantyhose. Panty was what the Queen

CHAPTER ONE

called him when she was feeling fond of him. When she wasn't feeling fond of him she called him 'that dratted boy'.

"Pelting the Abbot is one thing," said the Queen.

"Yee-uck!" The Prince pegged his nose between his fingers. "Didn't he stink?"

"He did rather, didn't he?" agreed the Queen. She allowed herself a little queenly snigger. The Abbot was not one of her favourite people; he would lecture her so! Also, he was grotesquely fat, which was because he ate too much.

7

(The Queen was as thin as a pin because of the disgusting dishes that Cook served up.)

"But seriously, Panty darling –," she patted the bench on which she was sitting. "I didn't so much mind you throwing bad eggs at the Abbot, but weren't you supposed to be doing your lessons?"

The Prince muttered something that sounded like "Bosh to lessons!" and sat down sullenly next to the Queen.

"But darling," said the Queen, "what kind of King will you be if you don't learn anything?"

"Why do I need to learn anything?" said the Prince. "If I'm to be King, others can learn for me.

CHAPTER ONE

Why should I have to bother? I shall simply tell people what to do, and they'll do it. And if they don't," he added, "I shall boil them in oil."

"Well, I suppose that is one solution," said the Queen, "though oil is quite expensive. And I have to say that your father has managed very well all these years without boiling anyone. That is because he attended his lessons. He didn't spend his time pelting people with bad eggs. Or running off down the hill to mingle with the Common Herd."

Prince Pantyhose grew rather red when the Queen said this. He hadn't realised that she knew.

"Oh, yes!" said the Queen. "I have heard what you get up to, and I very much wish that you wouldn't! It is not at all becoming.

Goodness only knows what you are likely to pick up!"

"But it amuses one," said the Prince (meaning himself).

"Well, for the future," said the Queen, "perhaps one could find something else to amuse one. I would rather you went and wallowed with the pigs in their sty than mingle with the Common People. Do I make myself clear?"

"As mud," muttered the Prince.

"I beg your pardon?" said the Queen, wondering if she had heard correctly.

"I said yes, absolutely," said the Prince.

CHAPTER ONE

The Queen looked at him, rather hard. She sometimes wondered what the world was coming to. Young people had not spoken to their parents like that when she was a girl.

"Very well, then." She gave him a little push. "Go off to your lessons and try to behave a bit more like a royal prince and a bit less like something that has crawled out of a dung heap!"

It was rather strong language for a queen to use – but honestly, there were times when Prince Pantyhose really did try her patience.

"Away with you!" she said. "Be gone!"

The Prince slouched off, muttering rude words. Having a queen for a mother was nowhere near as much fun as some people seemed to think. For that matter, being a prince wasn't all that much fun, either.

"I am quite sick of it," he said. "*Do this*, *do that* ... why, I'd enjoy myself more if I were a scullion!"

Chapter 2

It was morning and the castle was full of activity. Everyone, from the highest to the lowest, was bustling and busy. Kitchen maids were scouring, minions were scurrying, scullions scuttling to and fro. Knights and barons stalked the ramparts, courtiers chattered in the Great Hall. The Master of the King's Household, being old and doddery, was still pulling on his hose, but Cook had been up since the crack of dawn, making a mess of pottage and terrorising all the kitchen maids. Cook was in one of her tempers.

"Best keep out of her way," hissed the serving wenches, as they passed one another bearing plates of pottage – pottage for the knights and their ladies, pottage for the courtiers and the clerics, pottage for the King and Queen.

The Queen dumped most of hers in her chamber pot.

"So disgusting!" she said. "I do believe the creature picks her scabs and boils them."

The King said, "Very likely, my dear! Very likely," and went to empty his plate into the moat.

Now he was seated on the Royal Privy, pondering affairs of state, while the Queen was in her parlour, counting out her money. The Queen was rather fond of her money, which was one of the reasons she didn't sack the cook and find a better one. The King, for his part, was rather fond of sitting on his privy (otherwise known as the Royal Loo). The privy had only been installed a few weeks ago, so the King was still quite proud of it. It was the latest thing in privies! And such a simple idea.

"I wonder why no one ever thought of it before," said the King.

All it was, was a hole in the castle wall – up high, so no one could reach it from outside.

Inside there was a little ledge for the King to sit on, and a little alcove so that he could be private.

"Newfangled nonsense," sniffed the Queen. She didn't hold with such things. She had tried the new privy just once and had complained bitterly, saying that the ledge was cold to the Royal Backside. (Secretly, she was scared that someone coming up the hill might be able to see her nether regions.)

"But, my dear, it is such an improvement!" said the King.

It was true that when the wind came from a certain direction it tended to whistle round the Royal Bum Cheeks and cause goose pimples, but it was a great deal better than using a chamber pot behind a curtain. Chamber pots so quickly became filled up, and were all too easy to trip over. The King had had some embarrassing moments with chamber pots. Give him a newfangled privy any time!

On this particular morning he was sitting there, contemplating nature and enjoying the peace and quiet, and wondering to himself, in an idle kind of way, whether the peasants would revolt if he put up the taxes again, when he was rudely interrupted by the Queen running wildly in, with her crown all askew.

"My dear!" said the King. "What is it?"

"I was in the parlour," panted the Queen, "counting out my money –"

"Yes, yes? Put your crown on straight!"

"When Old Bottlenose came in." Bottlenose was the Queen's name for the Head of the Royal Household. "He told me –"

"Yes, yes? My dear, your crown!"

"He told me –" said the Queen.

"My dear, I do insist!" The King didn't very often insist, but it really upset him when his wife ran about the castle with her crown all crooked. He had his dignity to think of.

"Just a touch to the right," begged the King. "That's better! Now, tell me what's upsetting you?"

"It's that dratted boy!" shrieked the Queen.

"Pantyhose?" The King's heart sank. What had he done now?

"He's gone again!"

"Gone? Where?" said the King.

"Where do you think? Where he always goes!"

Where did he always go? The King knitted his brow – he knew he had to be careful. His wife was always accusing him of not paying attention when she spoke about the Prince and his bad behaviour. Where was it the boy was always going?

CHAPTER TWO

"Um ... down to the pig pens?" said the King, hopefully.

"Worse!" The Queen flung out an arm and knocked her crown sideways again.

"Worse?" mumbled the King.

"Far worse! He has gone to – mingle!"

"M-mingle?" said the King.

"Yes! Mingle. With the Common Herd!"

The King blinked. "With the cows?"

"With the people!" The Queen's voice rose to a screech. "He has gone to mingle with the people!"

"Oh, dear," said the King.

"Is that all you can say? *Oh dear?*" The Queen clutched at her crown just in time. "He will come back covered in vermin and smelling like a dung

heap. And all you can find to say is *oh dear!*"

The King sighed. He had been so happy, all alone in his alcove.

"I insist that you talk to him," said the Queen. "This time, Wyfrunt, I insist!"

Wyfrunt was the King's name. He was King Wyfrunt the Second. The Queen's pet name for him, when she was feeling tender, was Poopy Drawers. Right now, the Queen was obviously not feeling tender. She meant business!

"Very well, my dear." The King shifted the Royal Bottom on its ledge. (The ledge did have a nasty habit of cutting into the Royal Cheeks if one sat there too long.) "As soon as he returns, I will have a word."

"A stern word," said the Queen.

"Oh, very stern, my dear! I assure you."

Chapter 3

It was one of the Prince's favourite pastimes, to sneak off down the hill, disguised as a common person. He had his own special set of common clothes, which he kept in a secret hidey-hole, in the hollow trunk of a blasted oak which stood just outside the castle wall.

In his hidey-hole the Prince had an undershirt, which he had rubbed in the midden until it was brown and stinking; a jerkin which had once been green but was now grey and greasy and stained all down the front with droppings of food;

CHAPTER THREE

a pair of hose, all tattered and torn; and a pair of boots which were coming apart at the seams. On his way down the hill the Prince liked to roll himself in the dirt and pluck a few twigs to stick in his hair. That made him really feel like a common person!

Common people were, of course, quite disgusting. They cobbed and they hawked and they dropped their aitches. They never took baths or changed their clothes, their manners were frankly appalling, and they smelled simply dreadful, but the Prince reckoned they had a far better time of it than he did. Being a prince was *sooo* boring! *Do this, do that ... remember who you are ... attend to your lessons.* Nothing but slog, slog, slog! The call of duty. Set an example. Honour and obey and loads and loads of RESPONSIBILITY. It was all so tiresome!

He envied the Common People, who could do just as they liked, with no one but themselves to think of. Nobody told *them* to remember who they were, or to attend their lessons, or set an example. They didn't have to go on boring processions about the countryside, waving and nodding at crowds of unwashed yokels.

There were times when the Prince seriously thought he wouldn't mind being an unwashed yokel himself. After all, washing was a tedious business. So was getting dressed and undressed, even if he did have a Gentleman of the Bedchamber to help him. How much easier not to bother! To be as idle as one pleased. Free to have fun! To be a common person just for one day – or a week, or a month. Or as long as one felt like it! If he could just find someone to change places with him ...

CHAPTER THREE

"Hm …" thought the Prince, as he made his way down the hill. "I wonder …"

At the bottom of the hill was the market square, where all the Common People thronged together. This was where Prince Pantyhose liked to mingle. He saw a man roasting chestnuts over a brazier and his mouth watered. Roast chestnuts! How yummy!

So much tastier than Cook's mess of pottage. Unfortunately he was unable to purchase any as being a prince he naturally carried no money: other people always carried it for him. This was most vexatious! He really fancied a chestnut.

A boy was standing nearby. A boy about the Prince's age, with flaming red hair and freckles. (The Prince had flaming red hair and freckles.)

The boy was selling bundles of faggots, ready chopped for firewood. Suddenly, before the Prince's very eyes, the chestnut seller selected a monster chestnut, a chestnut the size of a pork pie, and offered it to the boy. The boy set down his bundles of faggots. He peeled open the chestnut and popped it into his mouth. He sucked. He savoured. An expression of bliss appeared on his face. The Prince's mouth watered more than ever. He felt a sense of outrage. This common boy was daring to eat a chestnut, while he, Prince Pantyhose, was forced to go without!

"Hey! You!" cried Prince Pantyhose.

"Me?" said the boy.

"Yes, you!" The Prince strode towards him. What right had a common boy to eat in front of a royal prince? What cheek! He'd have him boiled in oil. He'd have him hanged, drawn and quartered. He'd have his guts for garters!

He opened his mouth to say, "Spit out that chestnut!" Just in time, he remembered ... today he was not a royal prince. Today he was a common person.

"Want a bite?" said the boy, removing a piece of chestnut from his mouth.

"Um ... no! Thank you." The Prince took a hasty step backwards.

"Sure?" said the boy.

"Absolutely positive," said the Prince. "But jolly good of you to ask!" Really, the boy was quite a decent sort – for a common person.

He watched as the boy chewed on his chestnut. It seemed to the Prince that there was something strangely familiar about him.

"By golly!" cried the Prince.

"Something wrong?" asked the boy.

"You look just like one," said the Prince.

"One what?" said the boy.

"*One,*" said the Prince. "*Oneself!*"

It was true: the boy looked just like Prince Pantyhose!

"Extraordinary!" said the Prince.

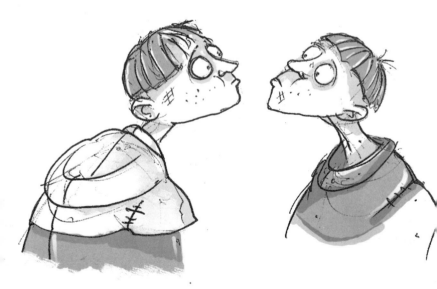

CHAPTER THREE

In fact, it wasn't extraordinary at all. The reason the boy (whose name was Jack) looked like Prince Pantyhose was that he was Prince Pantyhose's older brother. So naturally they looked alike; brothers often do.

Prince Pantyhose had never been told that he had a brother. It was a very dark chapter in the King and Queen's life and they preferred to forget about it. What had happened was this: when he was but a few months old, Prince Jack had been snatched from his cradle. He had been carried away by a common, rough fellow who had sent an ill-written ransom note to the King, demanding money.

> Yor Majisty,
>
> If yoo want yor sun bak in won peece, put 500 gold coyns in the blursted oak at the fut of the carstel warl.
>
> Do it in the mornin.
> URLY.
> Or else.
>
> Be warnd!!!

The King, in some distress, had shown the ransom note to the Queen.

"My dear!" he had said. "Just look!"

The Queen had looked – and had almost gone through the roof of the castle.

"Five hundred gold coins?" she had screeched. "Is this some kind of a joke?"

"I don't believe so, my dear. What do you suppose we should do?" The King had asked the question rather nervously. He knew how fond Queen Girdal was of her money. "Should we pay it, do you think?"

"At that price?" snarled the Queen. "Drat it, no! They can keep him!"

"But, my dear," the King had protested, "he is my son and heir!"

"So what?" said the Queen. "I'll have another one!"

Which, one year later, she did; which was how Prince Pantyhose came into the world.

As for the poor kidnapped prince, he was abandoned in the middle of a forest, where he was found, a few days later, by a woodcutter, who gave him to his sister, who sold him to a faggot seller who had five daughters and wanted a son to take over the faggot-selling business when he grew too old. Jack had lived with the faggot seller and his wife ever since. He had no idea that in reality he was a Royal Prince.

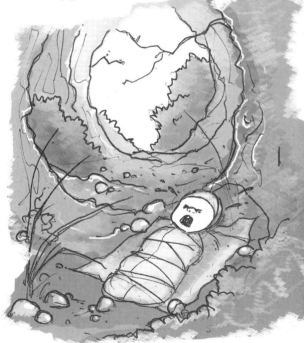

"I'll tell you what," said Pantyhose. "I've had a frightfully good idea! Why don't you and I change places? I live up there, you know." He flapped a hand towards the castle. "I'm Prince Pantyhose."

"Oh, yeah?" said Jack.

"Yah! Absolutely! I've got all my royal robes and stuff hidden in the trunk of a blasted oak. Just a short way up the hill. Come! I'll show you."

Needless to say, Jack didn't believe a word of it. Well, you wouldn't, would you? The son of King Wyfrunt and Queen Girdal, dressed in rags, hanging round the market square? Pull the other one! (As the saying goes.) Still, walking up the hill with a lunatic who thought he was a royal prince was a lot more fun than selling faggots, so Jack didn't argue but went happily trotting off. As lunatics went, this one seemed quite harmless.

"Jolly japes, eh?" said the lunatic.

"Yeah, great," said Jack.

Well! You can imagine his surprise when they reached the blasted oak and there inside, just as the lunatic had promised, was a bundle of royal robes.

"See?" said Pantyhose. "I told you! Now, you take me back and show me where you live, then you can come and get yourself all dressed up and pretend to be me. How does that strike you?"

"Yeah ... well! Okay," said Jack. "I guess I could give it a go.

How long d'you want me to be you for?"

"Oh! Just until one grows bored," said the Prince. "I should think one would be bored in about a week's time."

"Which one's one? You or me?" said Jack.

"Well, me, naturally," said the Prince. "I'm the prince! Now, kindly take me down and show me where you live."

"You'll have to sell my faggots," said Jack. "If you don't sell 'em, my pa'll whack you."

"One would be *delighted* to sell your faggots! But you can carry them," said the Prince, "until we get there."

Jack and the Prince walked back down the hill, across the market square, through a maze of winding streets, along a narrow alleyway. There, at the bottom of the alleyway, they came to a stop.

"That's it," said Jack. He pointed to a crumbling cottage; one of a row of crumbling cottages. The thatch on the roof was threadbare, the door hung half off its hinges.

"A hovel!" cried the Prince. "How utterly delightful!"

"You reckon?" said Jack.

"My dear fellow," said the Prince, "it's perfect! Quite perfect! One couldn't imagine anything more

squalid. I can't wait to get started. Off you go, now!" He gave Jack a little push. "Don't forget … you're Prince Pantyhose and I'm you. Right?"

"Yeah, sure," said Jack. "If that's what you want."

So that is how it came about that Prince Pantyhose went off to live in a hovel and sell faggots in the market place, while humble Jack went up to the castle to live with the King and Queen.

"Just for one week!" shouted the Prince.

Jack waved a hand. "Yeah, yeah! I hear you!"

Chapter 4

Life as a common person was not quite what Prince Pantyhose had expected. In fact, it would be true to say that it was a great disappointment, not to mention a rude shock.

He had known, for instance, that the hovel would be dirty, and also that it would be smelly. Common people were always dirty and smelly. But he had expected it to be warm and cosy!

It wasn't. It was cold and damp and totally DISGUSTING. To start with, there was only one room, and only one bed. This wouldn't have been so bad if the Prince had been able to have the bed to himself, but he wasn't allowed anywhere near it. The faggot seller slept on the bed, along with his wife, three of his daughters (the other two had got married and left home) and a squalling baby. The Prince had to sleep on a pile of mouldy straw in a corner, along with a couple of pigs,

who grunted and snorted all night long.

The pigs grunted and snorted, the faggot seller snored, the baby wailed, and the wind came whistling through the cracks in the walls. One night it rained and the rain came through the holes in the roof, so that the Prince woke up soaking wet. He had to stay soaking wet all day, as it seemed that Common People didn't own more than one set of clothes. They didn't even have a spare cloth that he could use for drying himself. They didn't have a cloth at all! The faggot seller had a sack, his wife had a piece of rag, and the daughters – Ethelburga, Ethelbun, and Ethelbred – had a few wisps of clean straw, which they guarded jealously for themselves.

"This be our straw," they said. "You leave off!" And they pushed the Prince away. They were big girls, and they were quite rough. Of course, they didn't know it was a prince that they were shoving. They thought it was a common person the same as themselves.

Poor Pantyhose was not used to such ungentle treatment. He stood miserably in a heap, shivering and shaking, while Ethelburga and her sisters just laughed.

"Yah, yer great ninny!"

"Gone soft, 'ave yer?"

"I shall catch a fever," moaned the Prince.
"Oh! Ketch a *feevah*!" said Ethelburga; and they all screamed.
"Ooja fink yew are? Prin Spanty Ose?"

It took the Prince a few seconds to work out what she was saying.
"Prince P-Pantyhose?"
"That nit!" said Ethelbun.
"Total nerd!" agreed her sisters.

"I say!" protested the Prince.

"Ay say!" echoed Ethelbun.

The Prince grew rather hot and red, in spite of being soaking wet. Did these women have any idea who they were talking to? He could have them boiled in oil!

At this point the faggot seller came over and told them to put a sock in it.

"And you!" He poked at the Prince. "Stop carrying on like a prat and shift your bum!"

The Prince was confused. What was the man talking about?

"I b-beg your pardon?" he said.

"Ay beg yer pahdn!" shrieked Ethelbred.

The faggot seller aimed a smack at her. "I said, put a sock in it!"

But she didn't have a sock, thought the Prince, more confused than ever. He wondered if perhaps the faggot seller were not quite right in the head.

"Well, go on! Get a move on!" The faggot seller picked up a bundle of faggots and thrust them at the bewildered Prince. "Get yourself out there, you idle lump!"

"B-but it's *raining*," bleated the Prince. "One will get wet!"

Ethelbred opened her mouth. "One will get –"

"Shut yer pie hole!" The faggot seller swung a

punch. Ethelbred ducked. "You! Lump!" He gave the Prince and his faggots a mighty heave in the direction of the door. "Get gone before I whack yer one!"

The Prince went. Fast. This was all most alarming! He was beginning to wonder if he might have made a mistake, changing places with a common person.

He had thought it would be such fun! Everyone knew the Common People had no manners, that they picked their noses (and probably their bottoms), and ate with their mouths open, but they were all jolly good chaps at heart. Salt of the earth, and so on. It was the simple healthy lives they led. Free of worry, free of care. No responsibility. No one but themselves to think of. Smelly and dirty, maybe; but *happy* in their smelliness and their dirtiness. He couldn't imagine what made the faggot seller so foul-mouthed and ill-tempered. What did the fellow have to complain of? He had a roof over his head, he had a bed to sleep in, food to eat (even if it had only been raw turnips for breakfast). What more did he want?

Sniffing (because he had no kerchief) the Prince made his way through the puddles of mud and piles of festering rubbish, to the market square. He had been looking forward to selling faggots!

He had thought it would be quite a jolly jape. But it rained all morning and most of the afternoon, and the Prince grew colder and wetter by the minute. It was all very well for the Common People, they were used to it. They probably enjoyed getting wet. They never washed, so they needed the rain to get them cleaned up. But the Prince wasn't used to it and he didn't enjoy it one little bit!

CHAPTER FOUR

He had told Jack to give him seven days before coming to check whether he had grown bored yet. Seven days of sleeping on damp straw and being shoved around by those dreadful women! Seven days of being called a prat and a booby and forced to eat raw turnips. How was he ever going to survive?

He could always go creeping back to the castle with his tail between his legs and confess what he had done – but the Queen would fly into the most dreadful rage. She might even box his ears. She could be every bit as bad-tempered as the cook when the mood took her. He couldn't go back to the castle! Not until Jack came, with his clothes.

Wearily, at the end of the day, Prince Pantyhose slopped his way homewards, back to the hovel, where it was the faggot seller who boxed his ears for not having sold enough faggots. The faggot seller's wife told him he was an idiot. "A total nincompoop!"

Ethelburga, Ethelbun and Ethelbred demanded to know what they were supposed to live on.

"Two bundles! How can you stand out there all day and sell only *two bundles*?"

"It was r-raining," pleaded the Prince. "There was n-nobody ar-round."

"Don't give me that!" screeched the faggot

seller's wife. "Stupid great lummock! Do something useful ... go and change the baby!"

Change the baby? "What would you l-like me to ch-change it for?" stammered the Prince.

"It's pooped itself, that's what I'd like you to change it for!"

"N-no, I meant ... what would you like me to ch-change it *for*?"

"Just change it, you great booby!"

Well, if that was what she wanted, thought the Prince. He couldn't help feeling it was a bit extreme. Changing one's baby, just because it had pooped. How brutal these Common People were!

CHAPTER FOUR

Gingerly, Prince Pantyhose slung the baby over his shoulder and set off along the lane. He hadn't gone far before he met a man with a chicken.

"I say, my good fellow!" He held out his bundle. "Would you care to change your chicken for this baby?"

Before the man could tell Prince Pantyhose to go jump in the nearest puddle, Ethelburga, Ethelbun and Ethelbred came charging up the lane.

"Wotcha fink yer doing?" yelled Ethelburga. "Give us that baby, yer great steaming nit!"

Ethelbun and Ethelbred both then boxed him round the ears (which by now were starting to feel

rather sore). Poor Prince Pantyhose had no idea what he had done wrong. They had told him to change the baby: he had tried to change the baby.

There was simply no understanding the ways of these common folk. All they did was whinge and moan. The man who sold chestnuts in the market square had been going on all morning about the unfairness of life, how some people were born rich while others were born poor. It seemed the King had just threatened to put up the taxes again. "And quite right, too!" thought the Prince. These people didn't know when they were well off. Fancy complaining about having to fork out a few more measly groats for the privilege of keeping a king and queen in their castle. They were lucky to have a king and queen!

"When I am King," thought the Prince, vengefully, "I shall put up the taxes tenfold, and anyone who complains will be boiled in oil!"

CHAPTER FOUR

That evening, for supper, the faggot seller's wife had made a stew of mangel-wurzels. It tasted even more foul than Cook's pottage, and it kept the Prince awake half the night with indigestion.

He felt very sorry for himself in the morning, but at least the sun was shining, and it was Sunday, so he would be able to have a lie-in. Oh! But what a shock ... it seemed the Common People didn't have lie-ins!

"Get your lazy lumping self out of that bed!" screamed the faggot seller's wife, kicking him in the ribs.

They surely couldn't expect him to sell faggots on a Sunday?

No: on a Sunday he was expected to go and chop wood to be turned *into* faggots.

"But what about church?" bleated the Prince.

"Since when," said the faggot seller's wife, "did the likes of us have time for church? That's for Them-Up-There, that is!" And she threw out a brawny arm in the vague direction of the castle. "Them as has the means to indulge their selves. Them as don't have to earn a living. Y'know your trouble, boy? You be getting ideas above your station, you be!"

So after a mouthful of raw turnips, the Prince went off to chop wood. He chopped all day, until his hands were rubbed raw and his back felt as if it were breaking in two. And then, when he was done, the faggot seller boxed his ears for not having chopped enough!

"Think this'll put bread in our mouths? You idle lummock!"

In all this time, the Prince never considered what a hard life the Common People led. It was only hard for him, because he was a prince. The Common People were born to it – and, in any case, they had only themselves to blame.

They didn't *have* to live in hovels and eat raw turnips. If they would only just shift themselves. Put a bit of effort into things.

But they didn't, because they were too idle.

The Prince fell on his nest of mouldy straw and went straight to sleep. It was the deepest sleep he had had in all his life. While he slept he dreamed. He dreamed of vats of boiling oil, all standing in a row. In the vats were the faggot seller, the faggot seller's wife, and the faggot seller's three daughters ... Ethelburga, Ethelbun, and Ethelbred.

CHAPTER FOUR

The only one he spared was the baby. But as for the rest of them ...

"Boil!" screamed the Prince, sitting bolt upright in his sleep.

* * * * *

Meanwhile, back at the castle ...

Chapter 5

The King gave Jack a good talking to when he turned up at the castle. He didn't really want to give him a talking to, but the Queen had said he must, and the King always did what the Queen said.

"Now, look here, Pantyhose!" The King wagged a finger.

Very meekly, Jack said, "Yes, sir."

The King was somewhat taken aback. *Pantyhose* being *meek*?

"Hrrrumph!" The King cleared his throat. "It's not good enough, you know. It will not do!"

Jack said, "No, sir," and cast down his eyes.

Extraordinary! What had come over the boy? He was actually showing a bit of respect for once in his life. Greatly encouraged, the King continued. "All this gallivanting about … running off down the hill to mingle with the Common People. It is not what one expects."

"No, sir. But it is such an excellent way of learning about them!"

"Eh?" said the King, startled. "Learning about them? Learning what about them?"

"Well, for one thing – sir," said Jack, still in respectful tones, "they are human beings just as we are."

Notice, by the way, that the minute he set foot inside the Castle – which was, of course, where he rightfully belonged – Jack began to act and speak just as a Royal Prince should. Who's surprised? He *was* a Royal Prince!

"Sir," he said, "the people suffer most dreadfully!"

"Really?" said the King. "How interesting! What do they suffer from?"

"Everything," said Jack. "Cold, and hunger, and –"

"Oh, that!" said the King. "Yes, yes, I know all about that! They should work a bit harder and stop being so idle."

"Sir," said Jack, "they are not idle! They work their fingers to the bone."

"So why are they cold and hungry? It makes no sense," said the King.

"The reason they are cold and hungry – sir," said Jack, "is that they have to pay such high taxes."

"Well, of course they do! How could we exist in the style to which we have become accustomed if the Common People did not support us? That, after all," said the King, "is what they are there for."

"But, sir," cried Jack, "you are killing them!"

"Is that a fact?" The King sat back on his throne and pulled, thoughtfully, at his beard. The Common People would be of no use if he had killed them all. "I was toying with the notion," said the King, "of actually putting the taxes *up*. I need a new carriage, and the Queen says her crown is getting tatty."

Jack remained silent. The King looked at him, pleadingly. "You don't think it's such a good idea?"

"Sir, I think it would be disastrous," said Jack. "I think if anything you should put the taxes *down*."

"What?" The King flared his nostrils. Beads of sweat broke out on his brow. What was the boy talking about, put the taxes down? The Queen would go demented!

"You would earn the undying gratitude of your subjects," said Jack.

The King began to feel rather ill. "Your mother would never stand for it," he mumbled.

"Would you like me to talk to her?" said Jack.

"Oh, my boy!" The King reached out and seized Jack's hand. "Would you?"

"No problem," said Jack.

The Queen was every bit as surprised

CHAPTER FIVE

as the King by this sudden change in her son's behaviour.

"Did your father have a word with you?" she said.

Jack bent his head. "He did, ma'am, and I am truly sorry."

The Queen blinked. "Oh," she said. "Are you?"

"I am," said Jack.

"Hm. Well! Just don't do it again."

"I won't, ma'am. You have my promise."

The Queen narrowed her eyes. Was this the Pantyhose she knew and loved? (It wasn't, of course, though he looked just like him.)

"Ma'am, you seem rather tense," said Jack. "Would it help if I rubbed your back for you?"

"Oh, if you would!" The Queen immediately arranged herself in a convenient position. She had been bent over a table, counting her money, all day, and her back was killing her. But since when had Prince Pantyhose ever cared?

CHAPTER FIVE

It was while he was rubbing the Queen's back that Jack introduced the subject of taxes.

"The People are finding it impossible to keep pace ... they are being asked to pay more and more."

"Yes, and very soon they'll be asked to pay even more," agreed the Queen. "Ooooh-aaah ... do that again! Just there, in the small of the back ... mmmm!" Delicious. Utterly delicious!

"I think you should put them *down*," said Jack.

"Do what?" said the Queen. "Don't stop, don't stop! Ooooh – mmmm – aaaah!"

"The taxes," said Jack.

"Mmmmmmmm!" said the Queen.

"I thought maybe, perhaps, we might post a proclamation in the market square?"

"Yes, yes! Post whatever you wish," said the Queen. "But just carry on with what you are doing!"

The following week, two servants rode down the hill and pinned a Royal Proclamation to the trunk of an old oak tree.

NOTICE be hereby given that as from today's date His Majesty, King Wyfrunt, out of the goodness of his heart and his love for his people, doth intend to lower the burden of their taxes by one groat per person. Long Live the King!

CHAPTER FIVE

The news spread throughout the length and breadth of the land, and there was great rejoicing. When the Queen got to hear of it, she came over quite faint and had to start counting her money all over again. The King, meanwhile, ran off to the royal privy with orders that he was not to be disturbed. He couldn't stand the thought of the Queen rushing in, with her crown all askew, screaming at him. Everyone in the castle waited for the Queen to start screaming. Everyone, from the lowest to the highest. The Queen's rage could be terrible to behold. But Jack went to speak to her. He told her how greatly beloved she would now be.

"Ma'am, you are the saviour of your people! You will be known as Girdal the Great, Girdal the Glorious."

"You think so?" said the Queen.

"Absolutely!" said Jack. "Which other queen in the whole of history has ever performed such a bountiful act?"

The Queen smirked. "I suppose it is rather bountiful."

"Ma'am, it is generosity above and beyond the call of duty!"

"Well, yes, I rather feel that myself," said the Queen. "Especially as my crown is getting so tatty.

I desperately need a new one."

"You are making a great sacrifice," said Jack.

The Queen agreed that she was, and felt rather smug. She liked the thought of being known as Girdal the Glorious. "I must go and tell the King," she said.

The King was still hiding in his privy. He cringed when the Queen came bursting in.

"My dear," he protested, "I gave strict orders –"

"Oh, bobbins to that!" cried the Queen. "I have important news … I am to be known as Girdal the Glorious!"

"That's nice," said the King, hoping that she would now go away and leave him in peace.

"We must have a banquet," said the Queen. "A banquet in my honour!"

"Why not?" said the King. Anything for a quiet life.

"And this time," said the Queen, "I intend to have *real food*. I deserve nothing less! I have performed a great and glorious act, above and beyond the call of duty. Pantyhose himself told me so."

"Why, in that case it must be true," said the King. He hadn't the faintest idea what the woman was talking about, but she seemed to be extraordinarily pleased with herself.

"I shall go and arrange it immediately!" said the Queen.

"Yes, dear." The King settled back, with a comfortable sigh. "You do that."

The King on his privy, the Queen arranging her banquet, Jack attending his lessons, as a good prince should. All was at peace, up in the castle. But down in the market square …

Chapter 6

Down in the market square, there was anything but peace. Prince Pantyhose had seen the proclamation, and he was most put out.

"It's that Jack! That imposter! That cheat!" Who else could have talked the King into such folly? *Lowering the taxes?* Whoever had heard of such a thing?

"I'm Prince Pantyhose!" screamed the Prince. "The one up there is a fake!"

Everyone in the market square turned to look at him. They all knew Jack, the faggot seller's son. Poor lad! He was obviously not feeling too well. Two strong men led him back home, where the faggot seller boxed his ears and the faggot seller's wife told him to pull himself together, while the three brawny sisters, Ethelburga, Ethelbun and Ethelbred, pinched his arms and tweaked his nose and told him he was a lump head.

"I'll have you boiled in oil!" screeched Pantyhose. "The lot of you!"

But the sisters just laughed and went, "Panty, Panty!" and tried to pull his stockings down.

For many days, Prince Pantyhose ranted and raved in the market square, trying to get someone to listen to him. But nobody would. In the end he became known as Poor Jack. He waited in vain for the real Jack to come and rescue him, but of course Jack couldn't. He had promised the King: no more gallivanting!

CHAPTER SIX

Little by little, as the days turned into weeks and the weeks turned into months, Prince Pantyhose was forced to give up and accept his fate. He had wanted to be one of the Common People, and now he was.

And so the years passed. Up at the castle, the Head of the Royal Household withered away until there was nothing left of him, while the cook had an apoplexy (brought about by ill temper) and all the scullions and the minions and the serving wenches breathed great sighs of relief.

The King and Queen grew old. The King spent more and more of his time on the royal privy, the Queen retired to her counting house to sort her money. She liked to arrange it in little piles across the floor. On her sixtieth birthday, Prince Jack, now known as Prince Pantyhose, bought her a new crown, which pleased her very much.

In the fullness of time, Jack became King. He was greatly loved. He only put up the taxes once during the whole of his long reign, and he never boiled anyone in oil. He was affectionately known as Panty to his grateful subjects, and went down in history books as Panty the Pleasant. To this day, a statue can be seen in his memory in the market square.

CHAPTER SIX

As for the real Prince Pantyhose, he eventually married a farmer's daughter and settled down quite happily to grow mangel-wurzels (at which he was rather good). He had sixteen children and thirty-two grandchildren, all with red hair and freckles. When he was an old man he liked nothing better than to tell his grandchildren how once upon a time he had been a royal prince and lived in a castle.

"A real castle, up on a hill. There was a moat, and a drawbridge, and I had my own pony to ride, and a feather bed to sleep in."

The grandchildren loved it! They didn't actually believe it, of course. Who would? It was just a made-up story. It couldn't possibly be true.

But it was true. And that is why, somewhere in the land, the great-great-I-don't-know-how-many-greats, but the great-great-*exceedingly*-great grandchild of a royal prince may be found in a school, in a class, at a desk … and may even be sitting next to you right now! That is the way things work out … sometimes!